THE LITTLE PRINCE

어린 왕자

두근두근 확장 영어 03

THE LITTLE PRINCE 어린 왕자

© 선진호 2021

초판 1쇄 인쇄 2021년 2월 3일
초판 1쇄 발행 2021년 2월 10일

원작 앙투안 드 생텍쥐페리 | **편저** 선진호
펴낸이 박지혜

기획·편집 박지혜 | **마케팅** 윤해승 최향모
디자인 this-cover | **일러스트레이션** @illdohhoon
제작 더블비

펴낸곳 ㈜멀리깊이
출판등록 2020년 6월 1일 제406-2020-000057호
주소 10881 경기도 파주시 광인사길 127 2층
전자우편 murly@munhak.com
편집 070-4234-3241 | **마케팅** 02-2039-9463 | **팩스** 02-2039-9460
인스타그램 @murly_books
페이스북 @murlybooks

ISBN 979-11-971396-8-0 14740
      979-11-971396-0-4 (세트)

* ㈜멀리깊이는 ㈜휴먼큐브의 출판유닛입니다.

두근두근
확장 영어 03

어린 왕자

THE LITTLE PRINCE

책장만 넘기면 문장이 완성되는 완벽한 어순 학습법

원작 앙투안 드 생텍쥐페리 **편저** 선진호

멀리깊이

"난 영어를 못해."

아마도 대한민국의 많은 영어 학습자들이 이런 생각을 하겠지만 의외로 여러분은 많은 양의 영단어를 알고 있습니다. 책상, 자동차, 나무, 하늘 등 눈앞에 보이는 대부분의 영어 이름을 알고 있을 정도니까요. 그럼에도 불구하고 영어가 어려운 이유는 뭘까요? 아마도 어순 때문이겠지요.

영어의 어순은 한국어와 정반대입니다. 이미 우리 머릿속에서 공고하게 완성된 어순 체계를 모두 해체해서 내뱉으려니 머릿속은 뒤죽박죽이 되어버리지요. 그러니 차근차근 영어 어순을 학습하는 과정이 반드시 필요합니다. 차근차근 한 단어씩 순서대로 늘려 나갈 수만 있다면 긴 문장을 말하는 일도 어려운 일이 아니게 됩니다.

두근두근 확장 영어 시리즈는 바로 이 어순을 완벽하게 학습할 수 있도록 구성했습니다. 책장을 넘기다 보면 어느새 긴 문장이 완성되어 있게끔요. 더욱 즐겁게 학습하실 수 있도록 한국인이 사랑하는 명작을 확장형 어순 프로그램에 맞춰 구성했습니다. 아마도 이 책을 모두 학습하고 나면, 원서 한 권을 읽은 듯한 감동과 뿌듯함을 느끼실 수 있을 거예요.

모든 확장형 문장이 듣고 빈칸을 채우는 딕테이션(dictation)으로 구성되었다는 것도 큰 장점입니다. 딕테이션만큼 몰입해서 학습하기에 좋은 방법이 없지요. 패턴이 길어지는 과정을 반복적으로 듣고 적는 훈련을 통해 자연스럽게 어순을 익힐 수 있을 겁니다.

여러분이 원서 속의 주인공들을 만날 생각을 하니 무척이나 설렙니다. 이 책이 여러분의 사랑을 듬뿍 받을 수 있도록 손을 모아봅니다.

2021년 선진호

Step 1 **책장만 넘기세요.**
문장이 저절로 길어집니다!

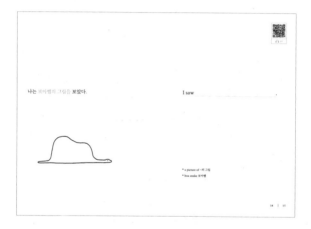

나는 보아뱀의 그림을 보았다.

I saw

• a picture of ~의 그림
• boa snake 보아뱀

14 | 15

❶ 모든 문장은 영어에서 가장 많이 쓰는 기본 패턴으로 구성했습니다. 책장을 넘길 때마다 영어의 어순대로 문장이 늘어나기 때문에, 우리말과 다른 영어 어순을 자연스럽게 익힐 수 있습니다.

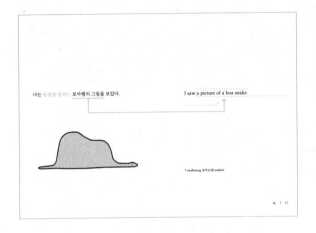

나는 동물을 삼키는 보아뱀의 그림을 보았다.　　　　　　　　　　I saw a picture of a boa snake

* swallowing 삼키는(원 swallow)

❷ 책장을 넘기면 앞 페이지에 있던 빈칸 문장이 자연스럽게 완성됩니다. 모르는 표현이 나와도 당황하지 마세요. 책장을 넘기면, 정답이 보입니다!

QR코드를 재생하세요.
저절로 문장이 완성됩니다!

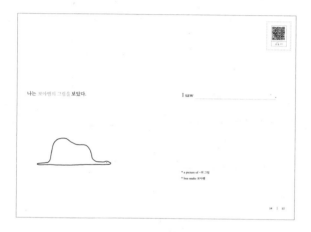

* 확장형 문장이 시작하는 모든 페이지에는 듣기용 QR코드가 있습니다. 자연스럽게 빈칸을 채우는 딕테이션(dictation: 들리는 대로 받아쓰기) 학습을 할 수 있어, 최상의 집중력으로 단기간에 어학 실력을 끌어올릴 수 있습니다.
* 스마트폰 카메라로 QR코드를 찍으시면 듣기 파일이 재생됩니다.
* https://cafe.naver.com/murlybooks 에 들어오시면 mp3 파일을 다운로드 받으실 수 있습니다.

Step 3 줄거리 문장을 읽으세요.
자연스럽게 원서 전체를 읽게 됩니다.

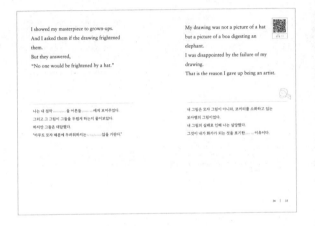

I showed my masterpiece to grown-ups.
And I asked them if the drawing frightened them.
But they answered,
"No one would be frightened by a hat."

My drawing was not a picture of a hat but a picture of a boa digesting an elephant.
I was disappointed by the failure of my drawing.
That is the reason I gave up being an artist.

나는 내 걸작 ......을 어른들 ......에게 보여주었다.
그리고 그 그림이 그들을 두렵게 하는지 물어보았다.
하지만 그들은 대답했다.
"아무도 모자 때문에 두려워하지는 ......않을 거란다."

내 그림은 모자 그림이 아니라, 코끼리를 소화하고 있는
보아뱀의 그림이었다.
내 그림의 실패로 인해 나는 실망했다.
그것이 내가 화가가 되는 것을 포기한 ...... 이유이다.

34 | 35

* 확장형 문장으로 패턴을 익힌다면, 줄거리 문장을 통해 원서 읽기의 기쁨을 느낄 수 있습니다. 모두가 알지만 누구도 읽어 본 적 없는 원서 읽기! 두 근두근 확장 시리즈로 경험해 보세요!

전문을 읽으세요.
두 배로 오래 기억하게 됩니다.

I saw a picture of a boa snake swallowing an animal and digesting it in a book when I was six years old. I drew my first drawing of a boa snake with a colored pencil. I showed my masterpiece to grown-ups. And I asked them if the drawing frightened them. But they answered, "No one would be frightened by a hat."

My drawing was not a picture of a hat but a picture of a boa digesting an elephant. I was disappointed by the failure of my drawing. That is the reason I gave up being an artist. Instead, I learned to fly airplanes to become a pilot.

So I lived my life alone, without anyone that I could really talk to, until I had an accident with my plane in the desert of Sahara, six years ago. On the first night, I went to sleep on the sand a thousand miles away from any of the villages.

"Draw me a sheep!" At sunrise, I was awakened by someone's little voice. I saw a very little boy, who stood there looking at me seriously. He seemed neither to lose his way, nor to be fainting from thirst. He repeatedly said, "Draw me a sheep."

Since I had never drawn a sheep, I drew for him a picture I had drawn so often. "I don't want an elephant inside a dangerous boa because everything is very small where I live."

So I drew several sheep, but he said all the sheep were not what he wanted.

I drew this drawing because I had to start taking my engine apart.

"The sheep you asked for is inside of this box."

"That is exactly what I wanted! Will this sheep need a great deal of grass? Because where I live, everything is very small..."

"Don't worry. It is a very small sheep."

* 본문에 등장한 확장형 문장과 줄거리 문장을 모은 전문으로 이제까지 익힌 필수 영어 패턴을 한 번에 정리할 수 있습니다. 출퇴근길이나 잠들기 전, 듣기 파일을 들으며 전체 문장을 소리내어 읽어 보세요. 긴 문장 말하기, 여러분도 해낼 수 있습니다!

CONTENTS

THE LITTLE PRINCE

나는 보아뱀의 그림을 보았다.

I saw _____.

* a picture of ~의 그림
* boa snake 보아뱀

나는 동물을 삼키는 보아뱀의 그림을 보았다.

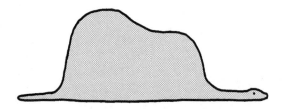

I saw a picture of a boa snake _____

_____ .

* swallowing 삼키는(원 swallow)

나는 동물을 삼키는 그리고 그것을 소화하는 보아뱀의 그림을 보았다.

I saw a picture of a boa snake swallowing an animal _____.

* digesting 소화시키는(원 digest)

나는 책에서 동물을 삼키는 그리고 그것을 소화하는
보아뱀의 그림을 보았다.

I saw a picture of a boa snake swallowing an animal and digesting it _____.

내가 여섯 살일 때, 나는 책에서 동물을 삼키는 그리고 그것을 소화하는 보아뱀의 그림을 보았다.

I saw a picture of a boa snake swallowing an animal and digesting it in a book _____
_____ .

여섯 살 때, 나는 책에서 동물을 삼킨 뒤 소화하는 보아뱀의 그림을 보았다.

I saw a picture of a boa snake swallowing an animal and digesting it in a book when I was six years old.

나는 내 첫 번째 그림을 그렸다.

I drew _____.

* drawing 그림

나는 내 첫 번째 보아뱀의 그림을 그렸다.

I drew my first drawing _____.

나는 색연필로 내 첫 번째 보아뱀의 그림을 그렸다.

I drew my first drawing of a boa snake_____

_____.

* colored pencil 색연필

나는 색연필로 내 첫 번째 보아뱀 그림을 그렸다.

I drew my first drawing of a boa snake with a colored pencil.

I showed my masterpiece to grown-ups.
And I asked them if the drawing frightened
them.
But they answered,
"No one would be frightened by a hat."

나는 내 걸작masterpiece 을 어른들grown-ups에게 보여주었다.
그리고 그 그림이 그들을 두렵게 하는지 물어보았다.
하지만 그들은 대답했다.
"아무도 모자 때문에 두려워하지는be frightened 않을 거란다."

03

My drawing was not a picture of a hat
but a picture of a boa digesting an
elephant.
I was disappointed by the failure of my
drawing.
That is the reason I gave up being an artist.

내 그림은 모자 그림이 아니라, 코끼리를 소화하고 있는
보아뱀의 그림이었다.
내 그림의 실패로 인해 나는 실망했다.
그것이 내가 화가가 되는 것을 포기한gave up 이유이다.

그 대신, 나는 비행기를 조종하는 것을 배웠다.

Instead, I learned _____.

* fly 조종하다, 비행하다
* airplanes 비행기

그 대신, 나는 조종사가 되기 위해 비행기를
조종하는 것을 배웠다.

Instead, I learned to fly airplanes _____

_____ .

* become ~이 되다
* pilot 조종사, 비행사

그 대신, 나는 조종사가 되기 위해 비행기를 조종하는 것을 배웠다.

Instead, I learned to fly airplanes to become a pilot.

그래서 나는 누구도 없이 홀로 내 삶을 살아왔다.

So I lived my life alone, _____.

* anyone 누구, 아무

그래서 나는 내가 진심으로 이야기할 수 있는 누구도
없이 홀로 내 삶을 살아왔다.

So I lived my life alone, without anyone _____

_____ .

* really 진짜로, 진실로
* talk to ~에게 말을 걸다

그래서 내게 사고가 있기 전까지 나는 내가 진심으로
이야기할 수 있는 누구도 없이 홀로 내 삶을
살아왔다.

So I lived my life alone, without anyone that
I could really talk to, _____

_____.

* accident 사고, 우연
* until ~(때)까지

그래서 내 비행기와 함께 내게 사고가 있기 전까지
나는 내가 진심으로 이야기할 수 있는 누구도 없이
홀로 내 삶을 살아왔다.

So I lived my life alone, without anyone that
I could really talk to, until I had an accident

———————————————— .

* plane 비행기

그래서 사하라 사막에서 내 비행기와 함께 내게 사고
가 있기 전까지 나는 내가 진심으로 이야기할 수
있는 누구도 없이 홀로 내 삶을 살아왔다.

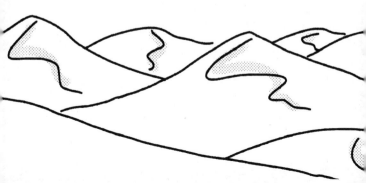

So I lived my life alone, without anyone that I could really talk to, until I had an accident with my plane _____.

* the Desert of Sahara 사하라 사막

그래서 육 년 전에 사하라 사막에서 내 비행기와
함께 내게 사고가 있기 전까지 나는 내가 진심으로
이야기할 수 있는 누구도 없이 홀로 내 삶을 살아왔다.

So I lived my life alone, without anyone that I could really talk to, until I had an accident with my plane in the desert of Sahara, _____ _____.

그래서 육 년 전에 사하라 사막에서 내 비행기와
함께 내게 사고가 있기 전까지 나는 내가 진심으로
이야기할 수 있는 누구도 없이 홀로 내 삶을 살아왔다.

So I lived my life alone, without anyone that I could really talk to, until I had an accident with my plane in the desert of Sahara, six years ago.

첫 번째 밤에, 나는 잠들었다.

On the first night, _____.

* went to sleep 잠들었다(원 go to sleep)

첫 번째 밤에, 나는 모래 위에서 잠들었다.

On the first night, I went to sleep _____

_____.

* sand 모래

첫 번째 밤에, 나는 1,000마일이 떨어진 모래 위에서
잠들었다.

On the first night, I went to sleep on the sand

                                       .

_____

* thousand 1,000

* away 떨어져, 떨어진 곳에

첫 번째 밤에, 나는 어떤 마을로부터도
1,000마일이 떨어진 모래 위에서 잠들었다.

On the first night, I went to sleep on the sand a thousand miles away _____

_____.

* village 마을, 부락

첫 번째 밤에, 나는 어떤 마을로부터도
1,000마일이나 떨어져 있는 모래 위에서 잠들었다.

On the first night, I went to sleep on the sand

a thousand miles away from any of the villages.

"Draw me a sheep!"

At sunrise, I was awakened by someone's little voice.

"내게 양_{sheep}을 그려줘!"

일출_{sunrise} 때에, 나는 누군가의 작은_{little} 목소리에 깨어났다_{awakened}.

I saw a very little boy, who stood there looking at me seriously. He seemed neither to lose his way, nor to be fainting from thirst.

He repeatedly said, "Draw me a sheep."

나는 진지하게seriously 나를 바라보며 서 있는 아주very 작은 소년을 보았다. 그는 길을 잃은 것 같지도, 갈증thirst으로 인해 기절할 것 같지도 않아 보였다.

그는 "내게 양을 그려줘."라고 되풀이해repeatedly 말했다.

나는 양을 그려본 적이 없기 때문에, 나는 그렸다.

Since I had never drawn a sheep, _____.

나는 양을 그려본 적이 없기 때문에,
나는 그를 위해서 그렸다.

Since I had never drawn a sheep, I drew _____

_____ .

나는 양을 그려본 적이 없기 때문에,
나는 그림 하나를 그를 위해서 그렸다.

Since I had never drawn a sheep, I drew for him

_____.

나는 양을 그려본 적이 없기 때문에, 나는 내가
그려봤던 그림 하나를 그를 위해서 그렸다.

Since I had never drawn a sheep, I drew for him

a picture _____.

나는 양을 그려본 적이 없기 때문에, 나는 내가 굉장히 자주 그려봤던 그림 하나를 그를 위해서 그렸다.

Since I had never drawn a sheep, I drew for him

a picture I had drawn _____ .

나는 양을 그려본 적이 없기 때문에, 내가 굉장히
자주 그렸던 그림을 그를 위해 그려주었다.

Since I had never drawn a sheep, I drew for him a picture I had drawn so often.

"나는 위험한 보아뱀 속에 있는 코끼리는 원하지 않아."

09

"I don't want an elephant _____
_____."

* inside ~안에
* dangerous 위험한

"모든 것이 매우 작기 때문에 나는 위험한 보아뱀 속에 있는 코끼리는 원하지 않아."

"I don't want an elephant inside a dangerous boa

."

"내가 사는 곳에서는 모든 것이 매우 작기 때문에
나는 위험한 보아뱀 속에 있는 코끼리는
원하지 않아."

"I don't want an elephant inside a dangerous boa

because everything is very small _____

_____."

* where ~한 곳

"내가 사는 곳에선 모든 것이 매우 작기 때문에 나는
위험한 보아뱀 속의 코끼리는 원하지 않아."

"I don't want an elephant inside a dangerous boa because everything is very small where I live."

그래서 나는 양 몇 마리를 그렸다.

10

So I drew _____.

* several (몇)몇의

그래서 나는 양 몇 마리를 그렸다. 하지만 그는
말했다.

So I drew several sheep, _____ .

그래서 나는 양 몇 마리를 그렸다. 하지만 그는
모든 양이 그가 원하는 것이 아니라고 말했다.

So I drew several sheep, but he said _____

_____ .

* all 다, 모든
* what ~한 것

그래서 나는 양 몇 마리의 그림을 그렸지만,
그는 모든 양이 그가 원하는 것이 아니라고 말할 뿐
이었다.

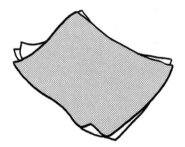

So I drew several sheep, but he said all the sheep were not what he wanted.

I drew this drawing because I had to start taking my engine apart.

"The sheep you asked for is inside of this box."

"That is exactly what I wanted! Will this sheep need a great deal of grass?

나는 엔진 분해apart를 시작해야 했기 때문에 이 그림을 그렸다.

"네가 요청했던asked 양은 이 상자 안에 있어."

"그게 바로exactly 내가 원했던 거야! 이 양에게 많은 양의great deal of 풀grass이 필요할까?

Because where I live, everything is
very small."

"Don't worry. It is a very small sheep."

"It's not that small. Look! He has gone to
sleep."

That was my first meeting with the little
prince.

왜냐하면 내가 사는 곳에선 모든 것이 너무 작아서……."

"걱정하지 마. 그건 아주 작은 양이거든."

"그렇게 작지도 않은데. 이것 봐! 양이 잠들었어gone to sleep……."

그것이 어린 왕자와의 첫 번째 만남이었다.

나는 그가 어디에서 왔는지를 배웠다.

I learned _____.

* from ~에서부터

나는 오랜 시간이 지난 후에야 그가 어디에서
왔는지를 배웠다.

I learned where he came from _____

_____.

* long time 오래

오랜 시간이 지난 후에야 나는 그가 어디에서
왔는지를 알게 되었다.

I learned where he came from after a long time.

"What is that object?"

"It is an airplane. It is my airplane."

"What! You dropped down from the sky?"

"Yes."

"저 물건_{object}은 뭐야?"

"이건 비행기야. 내 비행기지."

"뭐! 넌 하늘에서 떨어져 내려온_{dropped down} 거야?"

"응."

🎧 13

"So you, too, come from the sky!
    Which is your planet?"

"Do you come from another planet?"

He did not reply to my question.

"그렇다면 너도 하늘에서 왔구나! 어느 것이 네 별planet이야?"

"넌 다른 별에서 왔어?"

그는 내 질문에 대답하지reply 않았다.

나는 그 별이 약간 더 크다는 두 번째 중요한 사실을
배웠다.

I learned a second important fact _____

_____ .

* slightly 약간, 조금

나는 어린 왕자가 떠나온 그 별이 약간 더 크다는 두 번째 중요한 사실을 배웠다.

I learned a second important fact that the planet

was

slightly larger.

* came 왔다(원 come)

나는 어린 왕자가 떠나온 별이 집 한 채보다 약간 더
크다는 두 번째 중요한 사실을 배웠다.

I learned a second important fact that the planet

the little prince came from was slightly larger

_____ .

* than ~보다

나는 어린 왕자가 떠나온 별이 집 한 채보다 약간 더
크다는 두 번째 중요한 사실을 배웠다.

I learned a second important fact that the planet the little prince came from was slightly larger than a house.

어느 날 아침, 정확히 말해 해가 떠오를 무렵,

One morning, _____

_____,

* precisely 정확히

어느 날 아침, 정확히 말해 해가 떠오를 무렵,
장미 한 송이가 자신의 모습을 드러냈다.

One morning, precisely at sun rise, _____

_____.

* showed 드러냈다(원 show)

어느 날 아침, 정확히 말해 해가 떠오를 무렵,
눈부시게 아름다운 장미 한 송이가 자신의 모습을
드러냈다.

One morning, precisely at sun rise, a rose _____ _____ showed herself.

* dazzling 눈부신

어느 날 아침, 정확히 말해 해가 떠오를 무렵
눈부시게 아름다운 장미꽃 한 송이가 자신의 모습을
드러냈다.

One morning, precisely at sun rise, a rose with dazzling beauty showed herself.

"Forgive me. I'm still untidy. Ah! I'm hardly
   awake."
"Oh! How beautiful you are!"
"Am I not? I was born at the same moment as
   the sun.

"용서하세요_{forgive.} 전 아직 엉망이에요_{untidy.} 아! 전 아직 비몽
   사몽이에요_{hardly awake.}"
"오! 당신은 정말 사랑스럽군요!"
"그렇죠? 전 태양과 함께_{at the same moment} 태어났어요_{was born.}

I have a horror of wind. So, I want
you to put me under a glass globe
at night."

"Where you live is much colder than where I
came from."

전 바람은 질색_{horror}이랍니다. 그러니 밤에는 유리 덮개_{globe}로 저
를 덮어주었으면 좋겠어요."
"당신이 사는 곳은 내가 온 곳보다 훨씬 추워요."

그녀는 아는 것이 없었기에 **갑자기 말을 멈추었다.**

She suddenly stopped talking _____

_____ .

* since ~때문에, ~여서

그녀는 다른 세상에 대해 아는 것이 없었기에 갑자기
말을 멈추었다.

She suddenly stopped talking since she didn't

know anything _____.

* about ~에 대해
* other 다른

그녀는 여기에 왔기 때문에 다른 세상에 대해
아는 것이 없었기에 갑자기 말을 멈추었다.

She suddenly stopped talking since she didn't
know anything about other worlds _____

_____.

그녀는 씨앗으로 여기에 왔기 때문에 다른 세상에
대해 아는 것이 없었기에 갑자기 말을 멈추었다.

She suddenly stopped talking since she didn't know anything about other worlds because she came here _____.

* as ~로(서)
* seed 씨, 씨앗

그녀는 씨앗으로 여기 왔기 때문에 다른 세상에 대해
아는 것이 없었기에 갑자기 말을 멈추었다.

She suddenly stopped talking since she didn't know anything about other worlds because she came here as a seed.

그녀는 두세 차례 기침을 했다.

She coughed _____.

* times 회, 횟수

그녀는 어린 왕자를 몰아넣기 위해 두세 차례
기침을 했다.

She coughed two or three times

_____ .

* in order to (목적을) 위하여
* put 밀어 넣다, 놓다

그녀는 어린 왕자를 곤경에 몰아넣기 위해 두세 차례
기침을 했다.

She coughed two or three times in order to put the little prince _____ .

그녀는 어린 왕자를 탓하기 위해 두세 차례
기침을 해댔다.

She coughed two or three times in order to put
the little prince in the wrong.

어린 왕자는 점점 더 그녀를 믿지 않았다.

The little prince mistrusted her _____

_____.

* mistrusted 신뢰하지 않았다, 불신했다(원 mistrust)
* more and more 더욱더, 점점 더

장미꽃이 항상 아픈 척을 했기 때문에
어린 왕자는 점점 더 그녀를 믿지 않았다.

The little prince mistrusted her more and more

_____

_____.

* pretended to ~인 체했다(원 pretend to)
* sick 아픈, 병든

그녀가 이야기할 때마다 장미꽃이 항상 아픈 척을
했기 때문에 어린 왕자는 점점 더 그녀를 믿지
않았다.

The little prince mistrusted her more and more

because the rose always pretended to be sick

_____.

* every time ~마다

그녀가 어린 왕자에게 이야기할 때마다 장미꽃이
항상 아픈 척을 했기 때문에 어린 왕자는 점점 더
그녀를 믿지 않았다.

The little prince mistrusted her more and more
because the rose always pretended to be sick
every time she talked _____.

그녀가 어린 왕자에게 이야기할 때마다 아픈 척을
했기 때문에, 어린 왕자는 점점 더 그녀를 믿지
않았다.

The little prince mistrusted her more and more because the rose always pretended to be sick every time she talked to the little prince.

The little prince confessed to me one day.

"I shouldn't have listened to the flower."

"You must never listen to flowers, however hateful it is. You must look at them and smell them."

어린 왕자가 어느 날 나에게 고백한confessed 적이 있다.

"나는 꽃의 말을 듣지 말았어야 했어."

"아무리 얄미운hateful 말들이라도 꽃의 이야기를 들어서는 안 돼. 바라보고 향기를 맡아야 해."

20

"I didn't know how to enjoy when
my flower perfumed on my planet."
"I shouldn't have run away."
"I should have realized the tenderness
underlying her silly pretensions."

"난 꽃이 내 별에 향기를 뿜을perfumed 때 어떻게 즐겨야 하는지
알지 못했어."
"난 도망치지run away 말았어야 했어."
"난 그녀의 바보 같은silly 겉치레pretensions 아래
숨어 있는underlying 부드러움을 깨달았어야 했어."

그가 떠나던 날의 **아침에,**

On the morning _____,

* departure 떠남, 출발

그가 떠나던 날의 아침에, 그는 정돈했다.

On the morning of his departure, _____

_____.

* cleaned up ~을 치웠다(원 clean up)

그가 떠나던 날의 아침에, 그는 그의 별을 정돈했다.

On the morning of his departure, he cleaned up

_____.

그가 떠나는 날 아침, 그는 그의 별을 정돈했다.

On the morning of his departure, he cleaned up his planet.

그가 꽃에 물을 줄 때 그는 울 것만 같았다.

He felt like crying _____

_____.

* when (~하는) 때에
* watered 물을 줬다(원 water)

마지막으로 그가 꽃에 물을 줄 때 그는 울 것만
같았다.

He felt like crying when he watered the flower

_____.

* one last time 마지막으로

마지막으로 그가 꽃에 물을 줄 때 그리고 그녀를
유리 덮개로 덮어줄 때 그는 울 것만 같았다.

He felt like crying when he watered the flower
one last time _____

_____ .

* covered 덮어주었다(원 cover)

꽃에 마지막으로 물을 주고 유리 덮개를 덮어줄 때
그는 울 것만 같았다.

He felt like crying when he watered the flower one last time and covered her with glass globe.

어린 왕자가 작별 인사를 하는 동안
꽃은 기침을 하는 척했다.

The flower pretended to cough _____

_____ .

* say goodbye 작별 인사를 하다

어린 왕자가 그녀에게 작별인사를 하는 동안 꽃은
기침을 하는 척했다.

The flower pretended to cough while the little prince was saying goodbye _____.

어린 왕자가 그녀에게 작별 인사를 하는 동안 꽃은 기침을 하는 척했다. 하지만 그녀가 감기에 걸렸기 때문은 아니었다.

The flower pretended to cough while the little prince was saying goodbye to her, _____
_____ .

어린 왕자가 그녀에게 작별 인사를 하는 동안 꽃은
기침하는 척했지만 감기에 걸렸기 때문은 아니었다.

The flower pretended to cough while the little prince was saying goodbye to her, but not because she had a cold.

"I hope you to be happy," she told him at last.
He was surprised that she didn't say anything
that blamed him.

"Of course I love you. It was my fault that you
didn't know that I loved you. But you were
just as silly as I was. Put that glass globe
down."

"행복하기를 바라요."라고 마침내_{at last} 꽃이 말했다.

그는 그녀가 그를 비난하는_{blamed} 아무런 말도 하지 않아서
놀랐다.

"물론 전 당신을 사랑해요. 당신이 제가 당신을 사랑한다는
사실을 몰랐던 건 제 잘못_{fault}이었어요. 하지만 당신도
저만큼이나 어리석었어요. 그 유리 덮개는 내려놓아요_{put down.}"

"But the wind…"

"My cold isn't that bad. The night air
will do me good."

"But the animals…"

"I have to stand two or three caterpillars if I
want to know the beauty of butterflies.
Otherwise, who will visit me?"

"하지만 바람이…"

"제 감기는 심하지 않아요……. 밤공기도 제게 좋을_{do good} 거예요."

"하지만 동물들이……."

"만약 제가 나비의 아름다움을 알기 원한다면,
애벌레_{caterpillar} 두세 마리쯤은 참아야겠죠. 아니면_{otherwise} 누가
절 찾아오겠어요?"

"이렇게 서성이지 말아요."

"Don't hang around _____."

* hang around 서성거리다, 기다리다
* like this 이렇게

"당신이 마음을 먹었을 때 이렇게 서성이지 말아요."

"Don't hang around like this _____
_____."

* made up mind 속마음을 굳게 했다(원 make up mind)

"당신이 떠나기로 마음을 먹었을 때 이렇게 서성이지
말아요."

"Don't hang around like this when you made up your mind _____."

"떠나기로 마음먹었다면 이렇게 서성이지 말아요."

"Don't hang around like this when you made up your mind to leave."

그녀는 그가 보는 것을 원하지 않았다.

26

She didn't want him _____.

그녀는 그가 그녀가 우는 것을 보는 것을 원하지 않
았다.

She didn't want him to see _____.

그녀는 그가 그녀가 우는 모습을 보는 것을 원하지
않았다.

She didn't want him to see her crying.

그는 소행성 325, 326, 327, 328, 329 그리고 330을
방문하기 시작했다.

He began to visit _____

_____ .

* asteroid 소행성

그는 그의 이웃들인 소행성 325, 326, 327, 328, 329
그리고 330을 방문하기 시작했다.

He began to visit asteroids 325, 326, 327, 328, 329, and 330 _____

_____.

* which 어떤 것(들)
* neighborhood 이웃

그는 그의 견문을 넓히기 위해 그의 이웃들인 소행성
325, 326, 327, 328, 329 그리고 330을 방문하기
시작했다.

He began to visit asteroids 325, 326, 327, 328, 329, and 330 which were his neighborhoods ____

_____ .

* in order to 위하여
* broaden 넓히다
* knowledge 지식

그는 견문을 넓히기 위해 그의 이웃 소행성 325, 326, 327, 328, 329 그리고 330을 찾아가기 시작했다.

He began to visit asteroids 325, 326, 327, 328, 329, and 330 which were his neighborhoods in order to broaden his knowledge.

왕좌 위에 앉아 있는 왕

A king _____

_____

* throne 왕좌, 왕위
* who ~한 (사람)

소박하면서도 위엄 있는 왕좌 위에 앉아 있는 왕

A king who was seated upon a throne _____

_____

* simple 소박한, 간소한
* majestic 위풍당당한, 장엄한

소박하면서도 위엄 있는 왕좌 위에 앉아 있는 왕이
살고 있었다.

A king who was seated upon a throne which was
simple and majestic _____.

그중의 첫 번째에 소박하면서도 위엄 있는 왕좌 위에
앉아 있는 왕이 살고 있었다.

A king who was seated upon a throne which was simple and majestic lived _____

_____.

* of them 그중

소박하면서도 위엄 있는 왕좌에 앉은 왕이 그중
첫 번째 별에 살고 있었다.

A king who was seated upon a throne which was simple and majestic lived in the first of them.

어린 왕자는 장소를 찾기 위해 모든 곳을
둘러보았다.

29

The little prince looked everywhere _____ _____ .

어린 왕자는 앉을 장소를 찾기 위해 모든 곳을 둘러
보았다.

The little prince looked everywhere to find a
place _____.

* sit down (서 있던 사람이) 앉다

어린 왕자는 앉을 곳을 찾기 위해 여기저기를
둘러보았다.

The little prince looked everywhere to find a place to sit down.

하지만 왕의 옷에 의해 별 전체가 뒤덮여 있었다.

But the entire planet was covered _____

_____ .

* entire 전체의, 온
* covered by ~로 덮인
* clothes 옷, 의복

하지만 그가 입고 있는 왕의 옷에 의해 별 전체가
뒤덮여 있었다.

But the entire planet was covered by the king's
clothes _____ .

하지만 별 전체가 왕이 입고 있는 옷으로 뒤덮여
있었다.

But the entire planet was covered by the king's clothes which he was wearing.

So he remained standing upright, and he
yawned since he was tired.
"I forbid you to yawn in the presence of a king
  because it is a rude behavior to do so."
"But I can't stand a yawn."
replied the little prince.
"I have come on a long journey, and I have
  had no sleep…"

그래서 그는 그냥 서upright 있었고, 피곤해서 하품을 했다yawned.
"그것은 예절에 어긋나는rude 일이니, 왕의 면전에서 하품하는
  것을 금지하노라forbid."
"그렇지만 하품을 참을 수가 없어요." 어린 왕자가 대답했다.
"긴 여행long journey을 해서 잠을 자지 못했거든요……."

"Hum... Then, I order you to yawn
  right now."

But this time, the little prince said,

"I can't yawn anymore since you frightened
  me."

"Hum! Hum! Then I... I order you sometimes
  to yawn and sometimes to…"

He seemed to get angry.

"흠……. 그렇다면 지금 당장 하품을 할 것을 명하노라."

하지만 이번엔, "당신이 겁을 줘서 frightened 전 더 이상 하품을
할 수 없어요."라고 어린 왕자는 말했다.

"흠! 흠! 그렇다면 짐이… 명하니 어떤 때는 하품을 하고
  또 어떤 때는……."

그는 화난 기색이었다.

어린 왕자는 왕에게 물었다.

The little prince asked _____ .

어린 왕자는 왕에게 무엇을 통치하느냐고 물었다.

The little prince asked the king _____

_____ .

* ruled over 통치했다, 지배했다(원 rule over)

어린 왕자는 왕에게 그 조그만 별에서 무엇을
통치하느냐고 물었다.

The little prince asked the king what he ruled

over _____.

* tiny 아주 작은

어린 왕자는 왕에게 그 조그만 별에서 무엇을
통치하느냐고 물어보았다.

The little prince asked the king what he ruled over on the tiny planet.

"나는 내 행성을 포함한 모든 것을 통치한단다."

"I rule over everything _____.

_____."

* including ~을 포함하여

"나는 내 행성을 그리고 다른 행성들과 모든 별들을 포함한 모든 것을 통치한단다."

"I rule over everything including my planet, ____

_____ ."

"난 내 행성과 다른 행성들, 그리고 모든 별들을
포함한 모든 것을 통치한단다."

"I rule over everything including my planet, the other planets and all the stars."

어린 왕자는 해가 지도록 명령하는 것을 왕에게
부탁했다.

The little prince asked the king _____

_____ .

* older 명령하다
* set (해·달이) 지다

어린 왕자는 그가 궁금했기 때문에 해가 지도록
명령하는 것을 왕에게 부탁했다.

The little prince asked the king to order the sun

to set _____.

* curious 궁금한

어린 왕자는 왕이 해에도 명령을 할 수 있는지
그가 궁금했기 때문에 해가 지도록 명령하는 것을
왕에게 부탁했다.

The little prince asked the king to order the sun
to set because he was curious _____

_____ .

어린 왕자는 왕이 해에도 명령을 할 수 있는지가 궁금했기 때문에, 해를 지게 해달라고 왕에게 부탁했다.

The little prince asked the king to order the sun to set because he was curious if the king could even order the sun.

"Authority should be based on reason.
You should wait to see the sunset until
conditions are prepared according to my
order."

"권위authority는 사리에 근거를 두어야be based on 한다.
너는 일몰sunset을 보기 위해선 내 명령에 따라according to 조건이
준비될 때까지 기다려야 하느니라."

🎧 35

"When will that be?" asked the little
    prince.

"Hum! Hum! You will see how well
    my orders are obeyed in this evening about
    twenty minutes to eight."

"언제 그렇게 되나요?" 어린 왕자가 물었다.

"에헴! 에헴! 너는 오늘 저녁 7시 40분 정도에 내 명령들이
    얼마나 잘 지켜지는지(obeyed) 보게 될 것이다."

"내게 여기에서 할 무언가가 더 없기 때문에,"

"Since I have nothing more _____,"

"내게 여기에서 할 무언가가 더 없기 때문에,
나는 생각해요."

"Since I have nothing more to do here, _____."

"내게 여기에서 할 무언가가 더 없기 때문에, 나는
내가 지금 떠나는 것이 낫다고 생각해요."

"Since I have nothing more to do here,
 I think _____."

* had better ~하는 편이 낫다

"이제 저는 여기서 할 일이 없으니 지금 떠나는 것이
좋을 것 같네요."

"Since I have nothing more to do here,
I think I had better leave now."

하지만 한 신하를 가지는 것을 아주 자랑스럽게
여겼던 **왕은**

However, the king _____

_____

* was proud of ~를 자랑으로 여겼다
* subject (특히 군주국의) 국민, 신하

하지만 한 신하를 가지는 것을 아주 자랑스럽게
여겼던 왕은 원하지 않았다.

However, the king who was very proud of having

a subject _____ .

하지만 한 신하를 가지는 것을 아주 자랑스럽게
여겼던 왕은 그가 떠나는 것을 원하지 않았다.

However, the king who was very proud of having a subject didn't want _____ .

하지만 신하를 한 사람 가지게 된 것이 몹시
자랑스러웠던 왕은 그가 떠나는 것을 원치 않았다.

However, the king who was very proud of having a subject didn't want him to leave.

"Do not go. I will make you a Minister!"

"Minister of what?"

"Minister of Justice!"

"But there is nobody here to judge!"

"가지 마라. 너를 대신_{Minister}으로 삼겠노라!"

"무슨 대신이요?"

"사법_{Justice} 대신이니라!"

"하지만 재판할_{Judge} 사람이 아무도 없는데요!"

🎧 38

"Then I will order you to judge
yourself which is the most difficult
thing."

"But, I still do not need to live on this planet,
because I can judge myself anywhere."

The little prince was on his way with a sigh as
the king made no answer.

"그러면 가장 어려운 일인 스스로를 심판하는 일을
네게 명할 것이다."

"그래도 저는 여전히 이 별에 살 이유가 없네요,
저는 어디서든anywhere 저를 심판할 수 있으니까요."

왕이 답하지 않자, 어린 왕자는 한숨을 내쉬고는sigh 길을 떠났다.

"어른들은 정말 이상해."

"The grown-ups are _____."

"어른들은 정말 이상해."라고 어린 왕자는 자신에게 말했다.

"The grown-ups are very strange." _____

_____ .

"어른들은 정말 이상해."라고 어린 왕자는 그의
여행을 계속하면서 그 자신에게 말했다.

"The grown-ups are very strange." the little prince said to himself, _____

_____ .

* as ~하면서
* journey 여행, 여정

"어른들은 참 이상하군." 어린 왕자는 여행을
계속하며 속으로 중얼거렸다.

"The grown-ups are very strange." the little prince said to himself, as he continued on his journey.

찬양받기를 원하는 한 남자가 있었다.

There was a man _____
_____ .

* be admired 숭배되다

모든 다른 사람들에 의해 찬양받기를 원하는 한 남자
가 있었다.

There was a man who wanted to be admired ____

_____ .

두 번째 별에는 모든 다른 사람들에 의해 찬양받기를 원하는 한 남자가 있었다.

There was a man who wanted to be admired by all other men   .

* second 두 번째의

두 번째 별에는 다른 모든 사람에 의해 찬양받기를
원하는 한 남자가 있었다.

There was a man who wanted to be admired by all other men on the second planet.

"Ah! Ah! An admirer is coming for me!"

"Good morning, sir! That is a strange hat you
are wearing."

"It is a hat for greetings to people who
applaud me. But unfortunately, nobody at all
ever passes this way."

"아! 아! 나를 위해 찬양하는 사람admirer이 오고 있군!"

"안녕하세요, 선생님! 이상한 모자를 쓰고 계시는군요."

"이건 나에게 환호를 보내는 사람들에게 인사greetings를
하기 위한 모자라네. 하지만 불행히도 이리로this way
지나가는passes 사람이 아무도 없어."

The man said the little prince to clap
his hands.

The man raised his hat to greet as the
little prince clapped his hands.

남자는 어린 왕자에게 손뼉을 치라clap고 말했다.
남자는 어린 왕자가 손뼉을 치는 동안 모자를 들어 올리며
인사했다.

그래서 그는 그의 손뼉을 치는 것을 다시 시작했다.

So he began again _____.

* clap 박수를 치다, 손뼉을 치다

그래서 그는 보기 위해 그의 손뼉을 치는 것을 다시
시작했다.

So he began again to clap his hands _____ .

그래서 그는 그 남자가 그의 모자를 들어올리는 것을
보기 위해 그의 손뼉을 치는 것을 다시 시작했다.

So he began again to clap his hands to see _____

_____ .

* raise 들어올리다
* hat 모자

그래서 그는 그 남자가 인사로 그의 모자를
들어올리는 것을 보기 위해 그의 손뼉을 치는 것을
다시 시작했다.

So he began again to clap his hands to see the man raise his hat _____.

그게 재미있었기 때문에 그래서 그는 그 남자가
인사로 그의 모자를 들어 올리는 것을 보기 위해
그의 손뼉을 치는 것을 다시 시작했다.

So he began again to clap his hands to see the man raise his hat in greeting,

그래서 그는 그게 재미있었기 때문에, 그 남자가
인사로 모자를 들어 올리는 것을 보기 위해 다시
손뼉을 치기 시작했다.

So he began again to clap his hands to see the man raise his hat in greeting, because it was fun.

이러한 행동을 한 지 5분 뒤에

After five minutes _____

이러한 행동을 한 지 5분 뒤에
어린 왕자는 싫증이 났다.

After five minutes of this exercise _____

_____ .

* grew tired 싫증이 났다(원 grow tired)

이러한 행동을 한 지 5분 뒤에 어린 왕자는
그 장난에 싫증이 났다.

After five minutes of this exercise the little prince grew tired _____ .

이런 행동을 5분쯤 한 후에 어린 왕자는 그 장난에
싫증이 났다.

After five minutes of this exercise the little prince grew tired of the game.

그는 어린 왕자에게 그가 정말로 그를 존경하는지
물었다.

He asked the little prince _____

_____.

* admired 존경했다(원 admire)

그는 어린 왕자에게 그가 정말로 그를 많이
존경하는지 물었다.

He asked the little prince if he really admired

him _____.

그는 어린 왕자가 정말로 자신을 많이 존경하는지
물었다.

He asked the little prince if he really admired
him very much.

"What does 'admire' mean?"
"It means that you think me as the
   handsomest, the best-dressed, the richest,
      and the most intelligent man on this planet."
"But you are the only man on your planet!"

"존경한다는 게 무슨 뜻이죠?"
"그건 네가 나를 이 별에서 가장 미남이고 가장 옷을 잘 입고
   가장 부자고 가장 똑똑한intelligent 사람으로 생각한다는 것을
   의미하지."
"하지만 이 별엔 아저씨 혼자밖에 없잖아요!"

"Just admire me so that I feel happy."

"I admire you, but what does that
   have to do with you so much?"

"The grown-ups are certainly very weird." he
said to himself, as he continued on his journey.

"그냥 내가 기뻐할 수 있게 나를 존경해줘."

"아저씨를 존경해요. 그런데 그게 아저씨에게 무슨 상관이 있죠?"

"어른들은 확실히 정말 이상하군weird." 어린 왕자는 여행을 계속
하며 속으로 중얼거렸다.

어린 왕자는 알코올 중독자가 살고 있는 다음 별에
방문했다.

The little prince visited the next planet _____

_____ .

* alcoholic 알코올 중독자

어린 왕자는 잠깐 동안 알코올 중독자가 살고 있는
다음 별에 방문했다.

The little prince visited the next planet where
an alcoholic lived _____ .

* alcoholic 알코올 중독자
* for a short time 잠깐 동안

어린 왕자는 알코올 중독자가 살고 있는 다음 별에
잠시 방문했다.

The little prince visited the next planet where an alcoholic lived for a short time.

"What are you doing there?"

He silently sat down before a collection of bottles.

"I am drinking."

"Why are you drinking?"

"거기서 무엇을 하고 계세요?"

그는 병bottle 한 무더기를 앞에 놓고 말없이silently 앉아 있었다.

"술을 마시지."

"왜 술을 마셔요?"

"So that I may forget."

"Forget what?"

"Forget my shame of drinking all the time."

"The grown-ups are certainly very, very strange," he said to himself again.

"잊기_{forget} 위해서지."

"무엇을 잊기 위해서요?"

"항상_{all the time} 술 마시고 있다는 부끄러움_{shame}을 잊기 위해서지."

"어른들은 확실히 정말, 정말 이상하군."

어린 왕자는 다시 속으로 중얼거렸다.

너무 바쁜 한 사업가

A business man _____

너무 바쁜 그래서 그의 고개를 드는 것조차 하지
못했던 한 사업가

A business man who was so busy _____

_____

* raise 들어올리다, 들다

너무 바쁜 그래서 어린 왕자의 도착에도 그의 고개를
드는 것조차 하지 못했던 한 사업가

A business man who was so busy that he did not
even raise his head _____

_____

* arrival 도착

너무 바쁜 그래서 어린 왕자의 도착에도 그의 고개를
드는 것조차 하지 못했던 한 사업가가 네 번째 별에
살고 있었다.

A business man who was so busy that he did not
even raise his head on the little prince's arrival

_____ .

* fourth 네 번째의

너무 바빠서 어린 왕자가 도착했을 때도 고개조차
들지 않은 한 사업가가 네 번째 별에 살고 있었다.

A business man who was so busy that he did not even raise his head on the little prince's arrival lived in the fourth planet.

"Three and two make five. Five and seven make twelve… Phew! Then that makes five hundred and one million, six hundred twenty two-thousand seven hundred thirty-one."

"Five hundred million what?"

A business man kept calculating ignoring the little prince's question.

"셋에다 둘을 더하면 다섯, 다섯하고 일곱을 더하면 열둘……
휴우! 그러니까 5억 162만 2731이 되는군."

"무엇이 5억이에요?"

사업가는 어린 왕자의 질문을 무시한 ignoring 채
계속 계산 calculating 을 했다.

"Five hundred and one million what?"

"Millions of those little objects
in the sky."

"Ah! You mean the stars? And what do you
do with these stars?"

"Nothing. I own them."

"무엇이 5억 100만이에요?"

"하늘에 있는 저 작은 수백만 개 말이다."

"아! 별 말이군요? 그럼 그 별들을 가지고 뭘 하는 거죠?"

"하는 것은 없어. 그냥 소유하고_{own} 있지."

어린 왕자는 어떻게 그것이 가능한지 이해할 수
없었다.

The little prince couldn't understand _____

_____.

* possible 가능한

어린 왕자는 누군가가 어떻게 그것이 가능한지
이해할 수 없었다.

The little prince couldn't understand how it was possible _____ .

어린 왕자는 누군가가 그 별들을 소유하는 것이
어떻게 그것이 가능한지 이해할 수 없었다.

The little prince couldn't understand how it was possible for someone _____.

* own 소유하다

어린 왕자는 누군가가 하늘에 있는 그 별들을
소유하는 것이 어떻게 그것이 가능한지
이해할 수 없었다.

The little prince couldn't understand how it was possible for someone to own the stars _____ _____ .

어린 왕자는 하늘에 있는 별들을 누군가가 소유하는
것이 어떻게 가능한지 이해할 수 없었다.

The little prince couldn't understand how it was possible for someone to own the stars in the sky.

그는 그가 주인이라고 말했다.

He said _____.

* owner 주인, 소유주

그는 그가 그 별들의 주인이라고 말했다.

He said he was the owner _____.

그는 그가 첫 번째 사람이기 때문에 그가 그 별들의
주인이라고 말했다.

He said he was the owner of the stars _____

_____.

* the first 최초의 인물[것]

그는 그가 그들을 소유할 생각을 한 첫 번째
사람이기 때문에 그가 그 별들의 주인이라고 말했다.

He said he was the owner of the stars because
he was the first _____

_____.

그는 별들을 소유할 생각을 자신이 가장 처음
했으므로 자신이 별들의 주인이라고 말했다.

He said he was the owner of the stars because he was the first to think of owning them.

"Then what do you do with them?"

"I do something difficult such as counting and
recounting them. And I can also put them in
the bank."

"What does that mean?"

"그런데 아저씨는 별들을 가지고 무엇을 하나요?"

"난 그것들을 세어보고 다시 세어본다거나 recounting 하는
어려운 일을 하지. 그리고 그것들을 은행에 맡길 수도 있어."

"그게 무슨 말이에요?"

🎧 52

"That means that I write the number
  of my stars on a little paper. And then
  I put this paper in a drawer and lock it
  with a key."

"And that is all?"

"That is enough."

"그건 조그만 종이에 내 별들의 숫자를 적어 둔다는 말이지.
  그리고 난 이 종이를 서랍_{drawer}에 넣고 열쇠로 잠그지_{lock}."

"그게 다예요?"

"그거면 충분하지_{enough}."

"저는 꽃 한 송이와 화산들을 가지고 있어요."

🎧 53

"I own _____."

* volcano 화산

"저는 제가 물을 주고 청소하는 꽃 한 송이와
화산들을 가지고 있어요."

"I own a flower and volcanoes _____

_____ ."

"저는 제가 물을 주고 청소하는 꽃과 화산들을
 가지고 있어요."

"I own a flower and volcanoes that I water and clean."

"그건 내 화산들과 내 꽃에 유익한 일이에요."

"It is helpful _____

_____."

* helpful 도움이 되는

"내가 그들을 소유하는 것은 그건 내 화산들과 내 꽃에 유익한 일이에요."

"It is helpful to my volcanoes and my flower
_____."

"내가 그들을 소유하는 건 내 화산들과 내 꽃에
유익한 일이에요."

"It is helpful to my volcanoes and my flower that own them."

"하지만 아저씨는 별들에게 유익하지 않잖아요……."

"But you are not helpful _____..."

"하지만 아저씨는 별들에게 유익하지 않잖아요……."

"But you are not helpful to the stars…"

"어른들은 확실히 정말, 정말 이상하군."

"The grown-ups are _____ very, very strange."

* certainly 틀림없이, 분명히

"어른들은 확실히 정말, 정말 이상하군."
그는 혼자 속으로 중얼거렸다.

"The grown-ups are certainly very, very strange."

“어른들은 확실히 정말, 정말 이상하군.”

그는 여행을 계속하면서 혼자 속으로 중얼거렸다.

"The grown-ups are certainly very, very strange,"
he said to himself, _____

_____ .

"어른들은 정말 참 이상하군."
그는 여행을 계속하면서 혼자 속으로 중얼거렸다.

"The grown-ups are certainly very, very strange," he said to himself, as he continued on his journey.

The fifth planet which was the smallest of all was very strange. There was just enough room on it for a street lamp and a lamplighter. The little prince was not able to understand why there was a street lamp on this planet.

모두 중 가장 작은smallest 별인 다섯 번째fifth 별은 무척 특이한 별이었다. 그곳엔 가로등street lamp 하나와 점등원lamplighter에게 딱 맞는 공간이 있었다. 어린 왕자는 이 별에 왜 가로등이 있는지를 이해할 수가 없었다.

"I have to light my lamp and turn it
off every minute. The night comes
faster because this planet rotates faster
every year."
The little prince thought that the lamplighter
was stupid.

"나는 매분 나의 가로등을 켜고_{light} 꺼야_{turn off} 해요.
이 별이 해마다 더 빨리 회전하기_{rotate} 때문에,
밤도 더 빨리 찾아온답니다."
어린 왕자는 점등원이 어리석다고_{stupid} 생각했다.

하지만 어린 왕자는 그가 이 점등원을 좋아한다고
느끼기도 했다.

But the little prince also felt _____

_____.

하지만 어린 왕자는 그가 최선을 다하는 이 점등원을
좋아한다고 느끼기도 했다.

But the little prince also felt that he loved this lamplighter _____.

하지만 어린 왕자는 그가 그의 일에 최선을 다하는
이 점등원을 좋아한다고 느끼기도 했다.

But the little prince also felt that he loved this lamplighter who did his best _____.

하지만 어린 왕자는 그의 일에 최선을 다하는
이 점등원이 마음에 든다고 느끼기도 했다.

But the little prince also felt that he loved this lamplighter who did his best on his work.

노신사가 사는 여섯 번째 별

The sixth planet

* old gentleman 노신사

많은 책들을 쓴 노신사가 사는 여섯 번째 별

The sixth planet where an old gentleman _____

_____ lived

* wrote (책·음악 작품 등을) 쓰다, 집필하다(원 write)

많은 책들을 쓴 노신사가 사는 여섯 번째 별은
10배나 더 컸다.

The sixth planet where an old gentleman who wrote many books lived _____

_____ .

* ten times 10배
* larger 더 큰

많은 책들을 쓴 노신사가 사는 여섯 번째 별은
다섯 번째 별보다 10배나 더 컸다.

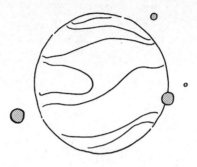

The sixth planet where an old gentleman who
wrote many books lived was ten times larger

_____.

많은 책들을 쓴 노신사가 사는 여섯 번째 별은
다섯 번째 별보다 10배나 더 컸다.

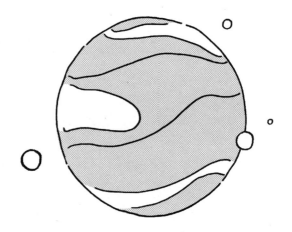

The sixth planet where an old gentleman who wrote many books lived was ten times larger than the fifth one.

"What are you doing?"

"I am a geographer."

"What is a geographer?"

"A geographer is a scholar who knows the location of all the seas, rivers, towns, mountains, and deserts."

"무엇을 하고 계세요?"

"난 지리학자geographer란다." "지리학자가 뭔데요?"

"지리학자는 모든 바다, 강, 마을, 산, 사막deserts의 위치location를 아는 학자scholar란다."

"Your planet is very beautiful.

　Does it have any oceans?"

"I can't tell you."

"Ah! Does it have any mountains?"

"I can't tell you."

"아저씨의 별은 정말 아름답네요. 바다_{oceans}도 있나요?"

"말해줄 수 없구나."

"아! 그럼 산은 있나요?"

"말해줄 수 없구나."

"And towns, rivers, and deserts?"

"I can't tell you that, either."

"But you are a geographer!"

"마을, 강, 사막은요?"

"그것 또한 말해줄 수 없구나."

"하지만 당신은 지리학자잖아요!"

"It is not the geographer who goes out to
count the number of the towns, the rivers,
the mountains, the oceans, and the deserts.
But we ask questions to explorers.
So, describe your planet to me because you
are an explorer who come from far away!"

"마을, 강, 산, 바다와 사막들의 숫자를 세기 위해
나가는goes out 것은 지리학자가 아니란다.
대신 우리는 탐험가들explorers에게 질문을 하지.
그러니 너의 별을 나에게 설명해다오describe,
너는 먼 곳에서 온 탐험가이니까!"

"그곳엔 오직 세 개의 화산과 꽃 한 송이가 있어요."

"There are _____

_____."

"그 별에는 오직 세 개의 화산과 꽃 한 송이가 있어요."

"There are only three volcanoes and a flower
_____."

"그 별엔 세 개의 화산과 꽃 한 송이가 있을
뿐이에요."

"There are only three volcanoes and a flower on the planet."

지리학자는 말했다. "난 기록하지 않아."

The geographer said, "_____."

* record 기록하다

지리학자는 말했다. "난 꽃과 같은 것은 기록하지 않아."

The geographer said, "I do not record _____

_____."

지리학자는 말했다. "난 그들은 아주 짧은 시간 동안 지속되기 때문에 꽃과 같은 것은 기록하지 않아."

The geographer said, "I do not record

something like flowers _____

_____ ."

"그것들은 아주 짧은 시간 동안만 존재하기 때문에,
꽃과 같은 것들은 기록하지 않는단다."라고
지리학자는 말했다.

The geographer said, "I do not record
something like flowers because they last a very
short time."

하지만, 어린 왕자는 왜 그가 꽃을 기록하지 않는지
이해할 수 없었다.

However, the little prince couldn't understand

.

하지만, 어린 왕자는 왜 그가 가장 아름다운 것인
꽃을 기록하지 않는지 이해할 수 없었다.

However, the little prince couldn't understand
why he didn't record the flower _____

_____ .

* most beautiful 가장 아름다운

하지만, 어린 왕자는 왜 그가 그의 별에서 가장
아름다운 것인 꽃을 기록하지 않는지 이해할 수
없었다.

However, the little prince couldn't understand why he didn't record the flower which was the most beautiful thing   .

하지만, 어린 왕자는 그의 별에서 가장 아름다운 존재인 꽃을 왜 그가 기록하지 않는지 이해할 수가 없었다.

However, the little prince couldn't understand why he didn't record the flower which was the most beautiful thing on his planet.

The little prince asked the geographer to give
an advice about the place to visit.
The geographer recommended the planet Earth
which had a good reputation.

어린 왕자는 지리학자에게 방문할 장소에 대한 조언advice을
요청했다. 지리학자는 좋은 평판reputation을 가진 지구를
추천해주었다recommended.

And the little prince went away,

thinking of his flower.

So then the seventh planet was the Earth.

그리고 어린 왕자는 그의 꽃을 생각하며 길을 떠났다.

그렇게 해서 일곱 번째 별은 지구였다.

어린 왕자는 그가 어떤 사람도 볼 수 없었기 때문에
매우 놀랐다.

The little prince was very much surprised

_____.

어린 왕자는 그가 막 도착했을 때 그가 어떤 사람도
볼 수 없었기 때문에 매우 놀랐다.

The little prince was very much surprised
because he couldn't see any people _____

_____ .

* just ~ 바로 후에

어린 왕자는 그가 지구에 막 도착했을 때 그가 어떤
사람도 볼 수 없었기 때문에 매우 놀랐다.

The little prince was very much surprised because
he couldn't see any people when he just arrived

————————————————.

어린 왕자가 지구에 막 도착했을 때, 어떤 이도 볼 수
없었기에 그는 매우 놀랐다.

The little prince was very much surprised because
he couldn't see any people when he just arrived
on the Earth.

무엇인가가 모래를 가로질러 움직였다.

66

Something moved _____.

* across 가로질러

그가 생각하기 시작했을 때 무엇인가가 모래를 가로
질러 움직였다.

Something moved across the sand _____

_____ .

그가 엉뚱한 별로 왔다고 그가 생각하기 시작했을 때
무엇인가가 모래를 가로질러 움직였다.

Something moved across the sand when he
started to think _____

_____ .

* wrong 엉뚱한, 잘못된

그가 엉뚱한 별로 온 것이 아닌가 생각하기
시작했을 무렵, 무엇인가가 모래를 가로질러
움직였다.

Something moved across the sand when he
started to think that he had come to the wrong
planet.

"Good evening."

"Good evening."

"What planet is this?"

"This is the Earth. And this is Africa."

"안녕."

"안녕."

"여긴 무슨 별이야?"

"이곳은 지구야. 그리고 여긴 아프리카이고."

67

"You are a funny animal."

"But I'm more powerful than the
finger of a king. I can take you somewhere
far away. I can send someone back to where
he came from." said the snake.

"넌 참으로 웃기게 생긴 funny 동물이구나."

"하지만 나는 임금님의 손가락보다도 더 힘이 세단다.
나는 너를 아주 먼 far away 곳으로 데려다줄 수 있어. 누군가를
그가 왔던 곳으로 돌려보낼 수 있지." 뱀이 말했다.

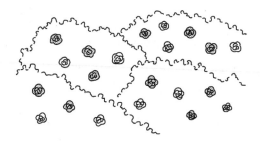

어린 왕자가 장미 정원에 다다랐을 때,

68

When the little prince reached _____

_____ ,

어린 왕자가 장미 정원에 다다랐을 때,
여우 한 마리가 나타나 말했다.

When the little prince reached the rose garden,

_____ .

* appeared 나타났다 (원 appear)

어린 왕자가 장미 정원에 다다랐을 때, 여우 한 마리가 나타나 "안녕."이라고 말했다.

When the little prince reached the rose garden,

a fox appeared and said, "_____."

어린 왕자가 장미 정원에 다다랐을 때,
여우 한 마리가 나타나 "안녕."이라고 말했다.

When the little prince reached the rose garden, a fox appeared and said, "Good morning."

"Who are you? You are very pretty. Come and
   play with me. I'm feeling so sad."
"I can't play with you because I am not
   tamed."

"넌 누구니? 정말 예쁘구나. 이리 와서 나와 놀아줘.
   난 너무 슬퍼feeling sad."
"나는 길들지tamed 않았기 때문에 너랑 놀 수 없어."

"What does 'tamed' mean?"

"It means to create ties."

"길들인다는 게 뭔데?"

"연결된 끈ties을 만드는create 거야."

"너에게, 난 한 마리의 여우일 뿐이야."

"For you, I am _____."

"너에게, 난 다른 여우들과 같은 한 마리의
여우일 뿐이야."

"For you, I am only a fox _____

_____."

* just 그저, 단지

"너에게, 난 네가 볼 수 있는 다른 여우들과 같은
한 마리의 여우일 뿐이야."

"For you, I am only a fox just like other foxes
_____."

"너에게, 난 네가 어느 사막에서나 볼 수 있는 다른 여우들과 같은 한 마리의 여우일 뿐이야."

"For you, I am only a fox just like other foxes you can see _____."

"너에게, 난 네가 이 별의 어느 사막에서나 볼 수
있는 다른 여우들과 같은 한 마리의 여우일 뿐이야."

"For you, I am only a fox just like other foxes
you can see in any desert   ."

"너에게, 난 이 별의 어느 사막에서나 볼 수 있는
여우들과 다를 바 없는 한 마리의 여우에 불과해."

"For you, I am only a fox just like other foxes you can see in any desert of this planet."

"하지만 우리는 우리가 서로를 필요로 한다는 것을
깨닫게 될 거야."

"But we will realize _____

_____."

"하지만 네가 나를 길들이면 우리는 우리가 서로를
필요로 한다는 것을 깨닫게 될 거야."

"But we will realize that we need each other
_____."

* once ~하자마자, ~할 때

"하지만 네가 날 길들이면 우린 서로를 필요로
한다는 것을 깨닫게 될 거야."

"But we will realize that we need each other once you tame me."

어린 왕자는 그 꽃이 그를 길들였다고 생각했다.

The little prince thought _____

_____.

어린 왕자는 그의 별에 있는 꽃이 그 꽃이 그를
길들였다고 생각했다.

The little prince thought that the flower had tamed him.

어린 왕자는 그의 별의 꽃이 그를 길들였다고
생각했다.

The little prince thought that the flower on his planet had tamed him.

"What do I have to do to tame you?"

"First, sit down a little away from me. You
will be able to sit closer bit by bit, day by
day.

"내가 널 길들이기 위해 뭘 해야 하지?"

"우선 내게서 조금 떨어져away 앉아. 넌 매일매일day by day
조금씩bit by bit 더 가까이 앉을 수 있게 될 거야."

🎧 73

And it would be better to come to
visit me every day at the same time.
If you come at four in the afternoon,
I will be happy from three."
That was how the little prince tamed the fox.

그리고 매일 같은 시간에at the same time 날 보러 오는 편이 더
좋겠어. 만약 네가 오후 네 시에 온다면, 난 세 시부터
행복해질 거야."
그렇게 해서 어린 왕자는 여우를 길들이게 되었다.

어린 왕자가 떠날 시간이 다가오자,

When the time comes _____

_____,

어린 왕자가 떠날 시간이 다가오자,
여우는 울 것 같았다.

When the time comes for the little prince to
leave, _____.

* seemed to ~할 듯 보였다

어린 왕자가 떠날 시간이 다가오자,
여우는 울 것 같았다.

When the time comes for the little prince to leave, the fox seemed to cry.

"I never wanted to do anything that could hurt
   you."
"Yes, of course."
"But you are going to cry! Then you got
   nothing out of it?"

"난 네게 상처 줄hurt 수 있는 일은 결코 하고 싶지 않았어."
"그래, 물론이지."
"하지만 넌 울려고 하잖아! 그럼 넌 아무것도 얻은got 게 없는
   거잖아?"

🎧 75

"I got something. Go look at the roses
again. You will be able to understand
that yours is the only rose
in the world."
The little prince went to the garden with
thousands of roses as the fox told him to.

"난 얻은 게 있어. 가서 장미들을 다시 봐봐. 넌 네 장미가
이 세상에서 유일한 존재라는 걸 이해하게 될 거야."
어린 왕자는 여우가 말한 대로 수천thousands 송이의 장미가 있는
정원으로 갔다.

"설령 사람들이 너희들과 내 장미를 구분하지
못하더라도,"

"Even if people can't distinguish _____

_____,"

"설령 사람들이 너희들과 내 장미를 구분하지
 못하더라도, 내 장미가 훨씬 더 소중해."

"Even if people can't distinguish between you and my rose, _____
_____."

"설령 사람들이 너희들과 내 장미를 구분하지
못하더라도, 너희들 모두보다도 내 장미가 훨씬 더
소중해."

"Even if people can't distinguish between you and my rose, my rose is much more precious

_____ ."

* combined 연합의, 결합의

"설령 사람들이 너희들과 내 장미를 구분하지
못한다 하더라도 내 장미는 너희를 모두 합한 것보
다 훨씬 더 소중해."

"Even if people can't distinguish between you and my rose, my rose is much more precious than all of you combined."

어린 왕자가 여우에게 돌아갔을 때,

When the little prince went back _____ ,

어린 왕자가 여우에게 돌아갔을 때,
그는 중요한 것은 보이지 않는다고 말했다.

When the little prince went back to the fox,

_____

_____

어린 왕자가 여우에게 돌아갔을 때,

그는 중요한 것은 눈에는 보이지 않는다고 말했다.

When the little prince went back to the fox,
he said that anything essential was invisible _____
_____ .

어린 왕자가 여우에게 돌아갔을 때,
여우는 중요한 것은 눈에 보이지 않는다고 말했다.

When the little prince went back to the fox,
he said that anything essential was invisible to
the eye.

"너는 오직 마음으로만 그것을 정확하게 볼 수 있단다."

"You can see it rightly _____
_____."

"너는 오직 마음으로만 그것을 정확하게 볼 수
있단다."

"You can see it rightly only with the heart."

내가 그를 처음 보았을 때, 나는 알지 못했었다.

When I saw him first, _____.

내가 그를 처음 보았을 때, 나는 그가 생각하고
있다는 것을 알지 못했었다.

When I saw him first, I didn't know _____

_____.

내가 그를 처음 보았을 때, 나는 그가 돌아갈 생각을 하고 있다는 것을 알지 못했었다.

When I saw him first, I didn't know he was
thinking _____ .

내가 그를 처음 보았을 때, 나는 그가 그가 왔던 곳으로 돌아갈 생각을 하고 있다는 것을 알지 못했었다.

When I saw him first, I didn't know he was
thinking of going back _____

_____.

내가 그를 처음 보았을 때, 나는 그가 장미를 다시 보기 위해 그가 왔던 곳으로 돌아갈 생각을 하고 있다는 것을 알지 못했었다.

When I saw him first, I didn't know he was
thinking of going back to where he came from

————————————————————— .

* see 보다

내가 처음 그를 만났을 때 난 그가 장미를 다시 만나기 위해 떠나온 곳으로 돌아갈 생각을 하고 있는지 알지 못했었다.

When I saw him first, I didn't know he was thinking of going back to where he came from to see the rose again.

"오늘 밤, 내가 여기 온 이후 일 년이 될 거야."

"Tonight, it will be a year _____

_____."

* since ~한 지, ~한 이후로

"오늘 밤, 내가 이곳에 온 지 일 년이 돼."

"Tonight, it will be a year since I came here."

"내 별이 내가 떨어졌던 그 장소 위에 있을 거야."

"My star will be just above the place _____

_____."

* fell 떨어졌다(원 fall)

"내 별이 작년에 내가 떨어졌던 그 장소 위에 있을
거야."

"My star will be just above the place where I fell
_____."

"내 별이 내가 작년에 떨어진 장소 바로 위에 있을
거야."

"My star will be just above the place where I fell last year."

I became very sad because I would never be
able to hear him laughing.
"If you love the flower on a planet, it will be
   happy to look at the sky in the night.
   Important things can't be seen."

난 그가 웃는 것laughing을 들을 수 없게 되어 매우 슬퍼졌다.
"아저씨가 만약 어떤 별에 있는 꽃을 사랑한다면, 밤하늘을
   바라보는 게 행복해질 거야. 중요한important 것은 보이지가
   않거든."

"Ah, little prince! I will miss your laughter!"

"I will be laughing from one of those stars up there. When you look up at the sky at night, you will be able to see stars that laugh."

That was our last talk.

"오, 어린 왕자야! 너의 웃음소리laughter가 그리울 거야!"

"난 저기 저 별 중의 하나에서 웃고 있을 거야. 밤하늘을 올려다볼 때, 웃는 별을 볼 수 있을 거야."

그것이 우리의 마지막 대화talk였다.

노란 빛 외에는 아무 것도 없었다.

There was nothing _____.

* nothing but 오직, 그저 ~일 뿐인
* flash 섬광, 번쩍임

그의 발목 가까이의 노란 빛 외에는 아무 것도
없었다.

There was nothing but a flash of yellow _____

_____.

* close to 아주 가까이에서

* ankle 발목

어린 왕자가 떠나던 밤에 그의 발목 가까이의 노란
빛 외에는 아무 것도 없었다.

There was nothing but a flash of yellow close to his ankle _____

_____ .

* in the night 밤중에

어린 왕자가 떠나던 밤, 그의 발목 가까이에서
노란빛이 반짝일 뿐이었다.

There was nothing but a flash of yellow close to his ankle in the night the little prince left.

그는 나무가 쓰러지는 것처럼 조용히 쓰러졌다.

He fell _____.

* gently 조용한, 완만한

그는 울지도 않고 나무가 쓰러지는 것처럼 조용히
쓰러졌다.

He fell as gently as a tree falls _____

_____ .

그는 울지도 않고, 나무가 쓰러지듯 조용히
쓰러졌다.

He fell as gently as a tree falls without crying.

모래밭이었기 때문에 **아무 소리도 나지 않았다.**

There was not any sound _____

_____.

* the sand 모래(사장)

모래밭이어서 아무 소리도 나지 않았다.

There was not any sound because of the sand.

I saw a picture of a boa snake swallowing an animal and digesting it in a book when I was six years old. I drew my first drawing of a boa snake with a colored pencil. I showed my masterpiece to grown-ups. And I asked them if the drawing frightened them. But they answered, "No one would be frightened by a hat."

My drawing was not a picture of a hat but a picture of a boa digesting an elephant. I was disappointed by the failure of my drawing. That is the reason I gave up being an artist. Instead, I learned to fly airplanes to become a pilot.

So I lived my life alone, without anyone that I could really talk to, until I had an accident with my plane in the desert of Sahara, six years ago. On the first night, I went to sleep on the sand a thousand miles away from any of the villages.

"Draw me a sheep!" At sunrise, I was awakened by someone's little voice. I saw a very little boy, who stood there looking at me seriously. He seemed neither to lose his way, nor to be fainting from thirst. He repeatedly said, "Draw me a sheep."

Since I had never drawn a sheep, I drew for him a picture I had drawn so often. "I don't want an elephant inside a dangerous boa because everything is very small where I live."

So I drew several sheep, but he said all the sheep were not what he wanted.

I drew this drawing because I had to start taking my engine apart.

"The sheep you asked for is inside of this box."

"That is exactly what I wanted! Will this sheep need a great deal of grass? Because where I live, everything is very small…"

"Don't worry. It is a very small sheep."

"It's not that small. Look! He has gone to sleep…"

That was my first meeting with the little prince. I learned where he came from after a long time.

"What is that object?"

"It is an airplane. It is my airplane."

"What! You dropped down from the sky?"

"Yes."

"So you, too, come from the sky! Which is your planet?"

"Do you come from another planet?" He did not reply to my question.

I learned a second important fact that the planet the little prince came from was slightly larger than a house. One morning, precisely at the sun rose, a rose with dazzling beauty showed herself.

"Forgive me. I'm still untidy. Ah! I'm hardly awake."

"Oh! How beautiful you are!"

"Am I not? I was born at the same moment as the sun. I have a horror of wind. So, I want you to put me under a glass globe at night."

"Where you live is much colder than where I came from."

She suddenly stopped talking since she didn't know anything about other worlds because she came here as a seed. She coughed two or three times in order to put the little prince in the wrong. The little prince mistrusted her more and more because the rose always pretended to be sick every time she talked to the little prince.

The little prince confessed to me one day. "I shouldn't have listened to the flower." "You must never listen to flowers, however hateful it is. You must look at them and smell them." "I didn't know how to enjoy when my flower perfumed on my planet." "I shouldn't have run away." "I should have realized the tenderness underlying her silly pretensions."

On the morning of his departure, he cleaned up his planet. He felt like crying when he watered the flower one last time and covered her with glass globe. The flower pretended to cough while the little prince was saying goodbye to her, but not because she had a cold.

"I hope you to be happy," she told him at last. He was surprised that she didn't say anything that blamed him.

"Of course I love you. It was my fault that you didn't know that I loved you. But you were just as silly as I was. Put that glass globe down."

"But the wind... My cold isn't that bad... The night air will do me good."

"But the animals..."

"I have to stand two or three caterpillars if I want to know the beauty of butterflies. Otherwise, who will visit me? Don't hang around like this when you made up your mind to leave."

She didn't want him to see her crying.

He began to visit asteroids 325, 326, 327, 328, 329, and 330 which were his neighborhoods in order to broaden his knowledge. A king who was seated upon a throne which was simple and majestic lived in the first of them. The little prince looked everywhere to find a place to sit down.

But the entire planet was covered by the king's clothes which he was wearing. So he remained standing upright, and he yawned since he was tired.

"I forbid you to yawn in the presence of a king because it is a rude behavior to do so."

"But I can't stand a yawn." replied the little prince. "I have come on a long journey, and I have had no sleep…"

"Hum… Then, I order you to yawn right now." But this time, the little prince said, "I can't yawn anymore since you frightened me."

"Hum! Hum! Then I… I order you sometimes to yawn and sometimes to…" He seemed to get angry.

The little prince asked the king what he ruled over on the tiny planet.

"I rule over everything including my planet, the other planets and all the stars."

The little prince asked the king to order the sun to set because he was curious if the king could even order the sun.

"Authority should be based on reason. You should wait to see the sunset until conditions are prepared according to my order."

"When will that be?" asked the little prince.

"Hum! Hum! You will see how well my orders are obeyed in this evening about twenty minutes to eight."

"Since I have nothing more to do here, I think I had better leave now."

However, the king who was very proud of having a subject didn't want him to leave.

"Do not go. I will make you a Minister!"

"Minister of what?"

"Minister of Justice!"

"But there is nobody here to judge!"

"Then I will order you to judge yourself which is the most difficult thing."

"But, I still do not need to live on this planet, because I can judge myself anywhere."

The little prince was on his way with a sigh as the king made no answer.

"The grown-ups are very strange." the little prince said to himself, as he continued on his journey.

There was a man who wanted to be admired by all other men on the second planet.

"Ah! Ah! An admirer is coming for me!"

"Good morning, sir! That is a strange hat you are wearing."

"It is a hat for greetings to people who applaud me."

"But unfortunately, nobody at all ever passes this way."
The man said the little prince to clap his hands. The man raised his hat to greet as the little prince clapped

his hands. So he began again to clap his hands to see the man raise his hat in greeting, because it was fun. After five minutes of this exercise the little prince grew tired of the game.

He asked the little prince if he really admired him very much.

"What does 'admire' mean?"

"It means that you think me as the handsomest, the best-dressed, the richest, and the most intelligent man on this planet."

"But you are the only man on your planet!"

"Just admire me so that I feel happy."

"I admire you, but what does that have to do with you so much?"

"The grown-ups are certainly very weird." he said to himself, as he continued on his journey.

The little prince visited the next planet where an alcoholic lived for a short time.

"What are you doing there?" He silently sat down

before a collection of bottles.

"I am drinking."

"Why are you drinking?"

"So that I may forget."

"Forget what?"

"Forget my shame of drinking all the time."

"The grown-ups are certainly very, very strange," he said to himself again.

A business man who was so busy that he did not even raise his head on the little prince's arrival lived in the fourth planet.

"Three and two make five. Five and seven make twelve… Phew! Then that makes five hundred and one million, six hundred twenty two-thousand seven hundred thirty-one."

"Five hundred million what?" A business man kept calculating ignoring the little prince's question.

"Five hundred and one million what?"

"Millions of those little objects in the sky."

"Ah! You mean the stars? And what do you do with these stars?"

"Nothing. I own them."

The little prince couldn't understand how it was possible for someone to own the stars in the sky. He said he was the owner of the stars because he was the first to think of owning them.

"Then what do you do with them?"

"I do something difficult such as counting and recounting them. And I can also put them in the bank."

"What does that mean?"

"That means that I write the number of my stars on a little paper. And then I put this paper in a drawer and lock it with a key."

"And that is all?"

"That is enough."

"I own a flower and volcanoes that I water and clean. It is helpful to my volcanoes and my flower that I own them. But you are not helpful to the stars… The grown-ups are certainly very, very strange," he said to himself, as he continued on his journey.

The fifth planet which was the smallest of all was very strange. There was just enough room on it for a street lamp and a lamplighter. The little prince was not able to understand why there was a street lamp on this planet.

"I have to light my lamp and turn it off every minute. The night comes faster because this planet rotates faster every year."

The little prince thought that the lamplighter was stupid. But the little prince also felt that he loved this lamplighter who did his best on his work.

The sixth planet where an old gentleman who wrote many books lived was ten times larger than the fifth one.

"What are you doing?"

"I am a geographer."

"What is a geographer?"

"A geographer is a scholar who knows the location of all the seas, rivers, towns, mountains, and deserts."

"Your planet is very beautiful. Does it have any oceans?"

"I can't tell you."

"Ah! Does it have any mountains?"

"I can't tell you."

"And towns, rivers, and deserts?"

"I can't tell you that, either."

"But you are a geographer!"

"It is not the geographer who goes out to count the number of the towns, the rivers, the mountains, the oceans, and the deserts. But we ask questions to explorers. So, describe your planet to me because you are an explorer who come from far away!"

"There are only three volcanoes and a flower on the planet."

The geographer said, "I do not record things like flowers because they last a very short time."

However, the little prince couldn't understand why he didn't record the flower which was the most beautiful thing on his planet. The little prince asked the geographer to give an advice about the place to visit. The geographer recommended the planet Earth which had a good reputation. And the little prince went away, thinking of his flower. So then the seventh planet was the Earth.

The little prince was very much surprised because he couldn't see any people when he just arrived on the Earth. Something moved across the sand when he started to think that he had come to the wrong planet.

"Good evening."

"Good evening."

"What planet is this?"

"This is the Earth. And this is Africa."

"You are a funny animal."

"But I'm more powerful than the finger of a king. I can take you somewhere far away. I can send someone back to where he came from." said the snake

When the little prince reached the rose garden, a fox appeared and said, "Good morning." "Who are you? You are very pretty. Come and play with me. I'm feeling so sad."

"I can't play with you because I am not tamed."

"What does 'tamed' mean?"

"It means to create ties. For you, I am only a fox just like other foxes you can see in any desert of this planet. But we will realize that we need each other once you tame me."

The little prince thought that the flower on his planet had tamed him.

"What do I have to do to tame you?"

"First, sit down a little away from me. You will be able to sit closer bit by bit, day by day. And it would be better to come to visit me every day at the same time. If you come at four in the afternoon, I will be happy from three." That was how the little prince tamed the fox. When the time comes for the little prince to leave, the fox seemed to cry.

"I never wanted to do anything that could hurt you."

"Yes, of course."

"But you are going to cry! Then you got nothing out of it?"

"I got something. Go look at the roses again. You will be able to understand that yours is the only rose in the world."

The little prince went to the garden with thousands of roses as the fox told him to.

"Even if people can't distinguish the difference between you and my rose, my rose is much more precious than all of you combined."

When the little prince went back to the fox, he said that anything essential was invisible to the eye.

"You can see it rightly only with the heart."

When I saw him first, I didn't know he was thinking of going back to where he came from to see the rose again.

"Tonight, it will be a year since I came here. My star will be just above the place where I fell last year."

I became very sad because I would never be able to hear him laughing.

"If you love the flower on a planet, it will be happy to look at the sky in the night. Important things can't be seen."

"Ah, little prince! I will miss your laughter!"

"I will be laughing from one of those stars up there. When you look up at the sky at night, you will be able to see stars that laugh."

That was our last talk. There was nothing but a flash of yellow close to his ankle in the night the little prince left. He fell as gently as a tree falls without crying. There was not any sound because of the sand.

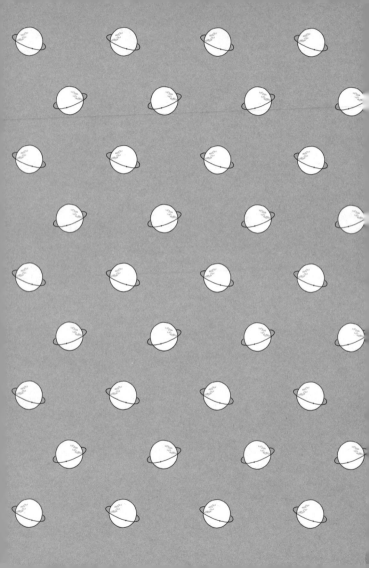